The
Narrow Road
to the
Interior

The
Narrow Road
to the
Interior

Kimiko Hahn

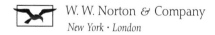 W. W. Norton *&* Company
New York · London

For information about permission to reproduce selections from
this book, write to Permissions, W. W. Norton & Company, Inc.,
500 Fifth Avenue, New York, NY 10110

Manufacturing by RR Donnelley, Bloomsburg Division
Book design by Charlotte Staub
Production manager: Julia Druskin

Library of Congress Cataloging-in-Publication Data

Hahn, Kimiko, 1955–
    The narrow road to the interior / Kimiko Hahn.—1st ed.
      p. cm.
    ISBN-13: 978-0-393-06189-5
    ISBN-10: 0-393-06189-2
    I. Title.
    PS3558.A32357N37 2006
    811'.54—dc22
                                        2006015316

W. W. Norton & Company, Inc.
500 Fifth Avenue, New York, N.Y. 10110
www.wwnorton.com

W. W. Norton & Company Ltd.
Castle House, 75/76 Wells Street, London W1T 3QT

1 2 3 4 5 6 7 8 9 0

for Miyako
to leaf through many years from now—

By nightfall, we come to Sōka, bony shoulders sore from heavy pack, grateful for a warm night robe, cotton bathing gown, writing brush, ink stone, necessities. The pack made heavier by farewell gifts from friends. I couldn't leave them behind.

—MATSUO BASHŌ, *The Narrow Road to the Interior*
translated by Sam Hamill

Contents

The
Narrow Road
to the
Interior

Compass

Dear L—

You asked for *a little compass*. Thank you!

I was looking for a definition of the zuihitsu from my shelf of Japanese texts, but discovered none gave more than a sentence or two. None seemed especially scholarly—which might be a good thing. None offered the sense of disorder that feels so integral. Here is what I did find:

> [L]iterally, "following [the impulses of] the brush," and consisting of brief essays on random topics
> —Donald Keene, *Seeds in the Heart*

> [Miscellany] . . . partly of reminiscences, partly of entries in diary-form
> —Arthur Waley, *The Pillow Book*

> [S]tray notes, expressing random thoughts in a casual manner
> —Makoto Ueda, *Principles of Classical Japanese Literature*, Earl Miner, ed.

Notice that none conveys the tonal insistence a writer finds her/himself in. None suggests an organizing principle—what we might call *a theme*. None comments on structural variety—list, diary, commentary, essay, poem. Fragment.

None offers that a sense of disorder might be artfully ordered by fragmenting, juxtaposing, contradicting, varying length or—even within a piece—topic.

From Mother seated at a window, winding her hair into a french-twist—to me, seated in a glass-bottom boat in a Tennessee cavern. Well—poor example.

Variety—e-mail, say. Gossip or scholarly annotation.

None states that these essays are closer to poetry—in my mind. That Saturn's rings might be fading—juxtaposed with a hula hoop. A hoop skirt. A pierced clitoris. Okay—for me, that the zuihitsu feels *encompassing*. That a fragment might be synecdoche, or excerpt. Or scrap. (Sappho comes to mind.) Why not!

(And when is a piece that resembles a fragment—really the whole?) What do you think?

Yours—K

Houston
August, 2005

Utica Station
Dep. 10:07 a.m. to N.Y. Penn Station

In the cavernous station, the train delayed for over an hour, I have watched a woman tend her newborn. She is tall, ties her hair back, has light dark skin and light, maybe green, eyes. Her baby is lighter; the man who picked up the ticket and kissed them, very black. I have watched her because her baby is so quiet. And I have not heard her voice.

On the train she sits one seat ahead and across the aisle. When the train brakes in Albany, the baby cries *ahh!* And she replies *ahh!* And I think, *just what I would do,* then feel miserable. *Was I* ever so attentive?

Placing one or the other child in the stroller, on the changing table, in a sassy seat, in the sandbox surrounded by plastic starfish and seahorses?

Stay. Come back.

She cradles the child, a boy by the blue; her rocking, syncopated with the train's chugging. Rain flecks the gray window. We pass a ditch of one hundred tires. A muddy lot of containers. Trees like sticks. A stray willow. We pass by the buds with such speed it could be late winter.

My heart is swollen, large as a newborn.

I do not want to return to their infancies. I would merely do the same: want to be in this notebook, not on the carpet covered with dolls. To be at the window waiting for their father, not swinging them in the park.

That was my mother—in the sandbox.

The farther south, the greener. Is it my imagination—or the proximity to the river?

I see a couple on a tiny jetty, holding a pink blanket.

My heart is swollen. As if a gland, not a muscle.

But I am wrong. There were stories I'd read and reread. *Mike Mulligan and His Steam Shovel. The Runaway Bunny. Ping, the Duck.* If I read "a big word," I'd explain as if the explanation were part of the narrative: *private*, one's very own; *escape*, get away.

There were evenings where we ate a picnic dinner on the Columbia lawns while their father worked late. I remember because when a plane roared over us, I'd say *plane plane* and she would look up to watch it roar away.

One of my first tasks was to name things. Then it became her task. One daughter's then the next. We'd walk from apartment to park— *Pizza. Doggie. Firetruck.*—naming things—*Daisy.*

Train. Bus. Car.

It is so difficult to travel with an infant—the bags of plastic things. One's own pockets, weighted with keys and change. Maybe a magazine stuck in somewhere. Balancing a cup of coffee with one hand, steering the stroller with the other. The baby struggling to be held. Difficult pleasures.

Writing time, remote.

I told myself then, *I need to slow down*—as if picking lice off a child's head. As if reading a poem—instead of sniffing around for the self on some meridian.

Along this train ride down the Hudson, the tracks run so close to the water it is as if the water were the rails.

I wonder if there is clay along the river's edge—just as Barbara and I found clay in the brook behind her house. Or as my daughters dug into the sand for the red clay on Fire Island, our hands afterward, cinnabar-red.

Always, *Mommy needs to—I need to—*

I look up from this notebook and see a tiny island with the shell of a castle—what is that? Is that how I've been a mother?

Dogwood blossoms, a cloud in the grove of branches.

A sailboat. A rowboat.

The mother and infant sleep now, the boy like a cat on her chest. Or as if her heart rested on the outside of her chest. I do recall that lovely pressure.

As we near the GWB, a tugboat towing a barge. Part of the bridge is wrapped in cloth. As if chilled.

I wish we didn't have to plunge into a tunnel.

Now forsythia. Now weeping cherry. I think of my mother—dead these past seven years—eight by Buddhist count.

The sudden brick landscape of Harlem. Then the tunnel, so now I see reflected in the window the boy who has been banging the seat, as if a sport. I need water to swallow an aspirin. I need to stretch.

My heart is swollen, as if—a hot water bottle!

The mother pats the baby. She begins to collect jackets for them both.

To put on an infant's jacket, I'd curl my own hand through the cuff and up the sleeve then pull her arm through. A tiny trick.

There was a difficult moment on a city bus: when I finally got the baby to stop stamping on the seat and sit down, the passenger behind me leaned forward and said, *You're a good mother.* I nearly wept.

Stay. Come back.

A mother with a fishing rod.

Looking for sensation on some meridian. In some station. Now speeding away from an acquaintance I might have asked, *shall I slip off my dress?* But I didn't. There was no urgency.

A mother with a plastic kite.

This is the difference: I don't find myself trailing a man around a room, screening gesture and tone.

This is the difference: I thought I was missing. Missing something.

As if a party balloon.

If my short hair didn't get so crushed I'd wear a baseball cap, too. (What would it say?)

Stay. Come back. Water. Pee-pee. You.

Before the tunnel—those dozen poles in the river—swollen and rotted from a long-vanished pier.

That's what the heart was—swollen—like a mother weeping for something. *A pier.*

Appear missing.

Opening Her Text

I nestle with my daughter in her bed in the room painted pink a decade ago; half the pink, now covered with glossy clippings of this or that star, male and female. Her reading light spots a book in my hands.

She is the oldest of two daughters and on the verge of one of those beginnings. Remove. Approach. (Reproach?)

Outside boys kill one another over sharp lyrics. Girls slash strangers across the face. In Prospect Park the fireflies begin their mating flares while other insects settle into moist foliage.

Each child was so large in the body I could barely recognize as my own; then each, so small in our hands. In our postpartum fatigue. Now this: the oldest leans against me to hear the first chapter of my favorite novel, written by a woman a thousand years ago.

⁂

She wants me to sit beside her, to hear me read *The Tale of Genji*—or maybe any book.

In the early pages Genji's mother is compared to Yang Kwei-Fei. The more jealousy she stirs up, the more the Emperor draws her to him in a spiraling first chapter.

An evil spirit strangled her? she asks. *That is so cool.*

It is cool to be so powerful. With the capacity to target. When I first read the Waley translation I was a sophomore at Iowa. I could not admit my own triangles—the roots so hidden from view. Mother, father, and sister were translated into one or another lover. Each became this Genji.

I see the roots of her own: *I don't want to go to her birthday party tomorrow. I'll be too jealous.*

That *what about me* is usually the younger one's exclamation.

＊

The younger one has rarely known a bedtime without a story about a small girl or talking animal—the older was then abandoned to read on her own. Tonight we can hear the boats in the harbor blow fog horns back into the fog. I didn't know the air had turned so damp. At this moment I want to be her, so someone can mother *me.*

I want hands on my face the way no husband or woman has ever held me.

＊

Genji is born, furthering the jealous undertow. When the mother dies the boy is passed from nurse to grandmother to a nurse closer to the father so the boy can be his memento. His search for the mother is a karmic draw.

＊

What of the moments that pull the mother away from the infant to the man?

Increasingly my daughter strays outside—the heart's curfew brings her back.

A curfew that will protect—what? Her own leave-taking?

＊

(I've already chosen for her the Seidensticker translation which I didn't read at first, having been raised on Waley's florid and more subjective prose. This, clear and clean. But also subjective, necessarily.)

What will she learn from my choices? From this narrative of longing and betrayal? This treatise on karma? Will she learn that jealousy is inherited? That I invent jealousies then arrange my escape?

Do I mean for her to admit this equation so deeply in her tissue that it takes constant calming—a cup of tea—a shot of bourbon—

a sleeping pill—

Do I seek out Genji—that lover, married lover, who holds me as if there is nothing else? Though many claim his heart by virtue of his promises, of his very tone. Do I need the *as if?* As if I exist in that Genji world where every relationship is more anxiety, more insecurity—than protection. Jealousy, a way of life?

(Can children sense this—)

Ah—my chest, my cage, my fear—

Who was Yang Kwei-Fei? she wishes to know. I read the footnote to get it right.

*

Did the women see each other's faces? Did all the women blacken their teeth? Did the men really believe the bride had horns?

What does she imagine a prince to be? One who has sex with everyone? Male and female? Should I say something about protection?

That the men control availability—have the women *wait on them?* Make the women hate one another, *compete?* Institutionalized uncertainty?

Do I fall for men not this girl's father—as fuel? As a tonic for the waiting? As a way to ruin? As a way to subvert some painful remnant?

It is so easy to abandon the self—as the lover becomes a constant daydream which life interrupts.

*

Once, after an hour of fucking I did cry out his name to which he responded, *You rarely say my name.* I never do. *It's a rule I've decided to break,* I tell him.

*

(Without a man in the house, with my attention mostly on girls, then what? What now that they prepare to squirm out of the nymph phase? Will we all wait for Genji?)

We have not yet gotten to the first wife, Aoi, a slightly older woman and important political match—and we have not gotten to his passion for his father's wife. Or Yūgao, Rokujō, Murasaki, Tamakazura—

*

Last night the sliver of moon was so thin it looked orange. And I wonder, how to grieve for the blackened part—that orange moon which is really mostly black?

*

If I can at least take care of a part of her perhaps she will learn to see her self as more than a point of departure. Perhaps she will see that a woman loves her, so she can *become a woman.*

Those women waited in boxes of semidarkness, complexions pale as daikon, for the men sending lines of poetry, sprays of cherries— sent the morning after—

The summer heat rises this spring from park lawn and sewer. I wish I could return to the winter when my breath, opaque as a ghost, betrayed my desire for him as he held me. The air that froze that evening in the parking lot.

Where is the institutionalized form of expressing jealousy—as in Morris's footnote on Genji? Institutionalized *uncertainty.*

*

Yūgao didn't stand a chance—birthing a girl child with Genji's best friend only inspired his interest further; allying herself with Genji assured death by an evil spirit. Didn't he wed that girl child in the end—

I love who I am in that dark room lit with twilight—like Genji. But why? Why now?

Where is jealousy in my own strategies—common as those books from his past lovers—from which I rip out the dedication pages?

Common as the taste of childhood—red lipstick, my mother telling me to open my mouth very wide so she could apply the red evenly and I could look beautiful, too.

*

The girls do not realize how deeply unhappy I am—but not *with* them.

What about my body that I was determined to love—that would not belong to me, somehow, until my fortieth birthday when I bid my youth farewell.

Now my daughter's body begins to swell with hormonal confusions—delighted and sacred.

*

sacred not *scared*—

*

She seems thirsty for me to read to her—should I switch out of the abridged?

The younger daughter sits on my bed as I grade papers early one evening after mac-and-cheese. I put them aside and we look up at the wall where I've hung prints depicting several Genji chapters. *That one,* I point to the second, *is when Genji is courting his best friend's former lover. He loves her. But another lover—an older and married woman—is extremely jealous. She sends her spirit out to kill this younger one. That is the scene where she is murdered.* It seems almost believable.

I love those pictures, she says. *Sometimes I lie on your bed and stare at each one.*

Cuts from the Zuihitsu on My Daughter

Recalling that self that dressed the way my daughter now wishes to dress—in as little as possible. Layers in order to get out of the house.

[A skimpy crochetted thing.] [A velvet black V-neck dress. Floor-length. Thrift-shop scented. Worn through mid-June. 1972?]

1972

I can't imagine getting a facial—sitting for an hour with someone tending my face: massaging, steaming, slathering creams, rinsing—I tear when I just get a manicure. But lying back with my eyes closed would be unbearable. So much pleasure.

How to claim what was lost decades ago so as to teach her it is possible to be—what?

the steam

the esteem

to wear those transparent blouses—

Expensive lipstick tastes so plush, the taste of Mother and her attention when Meg and I played dress-up. Squabbling over high heels.

A little consideration makes me weep and I tell her, *I appreciate that thanks for remembering soy milk at the market*—though I know this is my responsibility.

[tasks]

Just nineteen I sat on my parents' bed to tell them something I'd been trying to say for nearly six months—that I'd had an abortion. I wanted them to know, felt they should know, would want to. Then Mother wanted to know, asked, *how could you be so stupid* and Father tried to quiet her.

No one asked, Did it hurt—*yes*. Was I frightened—*terrified*. Had I gone alone—*no*.

The toughest is protecting her from my poetry.

Tie-dyed bikini and love beads, 1968. The red star, 1976.

My daughters are so awkwardly lovely that I am afraid to stare unless they are in sleep. When I do, I wonder, will they turn into a soft animal—will they run away?

(Then there was the Escalation.)

rinsing her long auburn hair in the sink

the sink

Wellfleet, Midsummer

(2000)

1

In midsummer heat when I cannot sit in one chair for more than a
few moments, like Shikishi, *I feel sad for no reason.*

2

Dozing in the grass, I wish I had paid attention to my mother: I
cannot distinguish one birdcall from another.

9

In a room overlooking pine, I stop thinking of Mother's death and
think of my lover's hands only to recall Mother brushing knots
from my hair.

5

Far from the former husband, this rain-soaked marsh is where I
know a downpour will last. And the lover's *breadth.*

6

From my bedroom, branches of pine are white, blanketed with
ancient lichen. If we are as fortunate.

7

On the third day of rain—nature from indoors is without a scent,
even ozone. All—excepting his humidity.

10

At low tide this marsh pools around the road, the vein from the
illicit cottage to the unfeeling world.

8

It is the heart-that-is-afraid-to-be-heard, this bridge over the salt
marsh at high tide. Still—it is passable—

3

He picks up a box turtle in the middle of the road. He's fifty-two
but believes it will bring childhood back in a box.

11

The tide pulls out and the grasses simmer alive in the twilight. If my
heart were only this marsh!

12

From grasses fretting with oysters and crabs, the mud stutters and I
can tell you wait for another dusk to ask me. And I am not
impatient.

13

At low tide the water empties below the service road and the mud
twitches with seven kinds of crab. Now you can leave but won't.

14

At dawn, wading in the bay's shallows, I am pinched by something
sharp—I still feel beside myself.

15

Do not think of the past for a moment—except for the tree my daughter
planted from a lemon seed when her grandmother was living.

16

Insect cries cannot compete with his single-finger touch-typing. Or perhaps, this midmorning, it's my hearing.

19

Where have the geese gone? I wonder this in the corona of my lover's sleep—as Princess Shikishi wondered the same from her vestal services.

20

He cares for me so much he buys a slice of mudpie then scolds me for eating it. Is it early summer! So what!

22

In the tidal pool a half dozen hermit crabs scuffle over an empty shell which the largest wins but cannot fit into. *That.*

Radio and Mirror

responding to Abe Kobo's *Suna no onna [Woman in the Dunes]*

iv.

She took in a stray that clearly had been beaten: slipping off her belt to undress or picking up an umbrella, the dog would piss all over. Eventually the dog stopped. She hated hats, too.

In the park the dog would chase another dog in a huge circle faster then slower so the other dog became the chaser. She'd laugh at the thrill on her animal's face.

i.

She asks herself: *Is it that I can't stay here or that I need to leave? I've been looking for a choice that does not admit craving. Even so, I love that he loves insects.*

She got up and turned on the television. Curled up in the chair. Picked up the phone, pushed memory #2, then pressed the tv *mute* so she could hear her friend. No answer so she got up and rubbed lotion onto her face, elbows, knees—those rough or sagging moments of her body. She picked up the remote.

v.

She writes in a notebook: *I dream or at least recall dreams when I am away from home. On a month-long summer holiday I have nightmares the first week. In each I find things under my pillow: severed hand, bloody teeth, vomit-sodden blouse—but whose blouse?*

She couldn't breathe in to scream out.

vi. ["In the black splotch of his vomit . . ."]

Same notebook, different entry: *I threw up in the bathtub again and
again. Shuddered.*
Shuttered.

vii. ["The sounds of shovel . . ."]

She loves the sound of crackling oil.

When she heard her neighbor's manual typewriter she would begin
to type poems also. Her best poem, on her mother retelling the
peach story, was written around 2 a.m. one such night.

iii.

She bathes in the sand like a bird or rabbit.

She recalled bathing with her grandmother in the *ofuro:* the soap
rinsed off with buckets of water outside the tub then crouching
lazily in the steaming water. Her grandmother's breasts, dry looking.
Interesting and dry looking. She recalled a shower with a lover:
how the water would suddenly scald so he would turn her away
from the spray until the temperature cooled again. The protection.
She recalled a dog rolling in the sand. A bird fluttering in dust.
Children in a playpen of colorful Ping-Pong balls. She recalled see-
ing her mother in the bath one sultry afternoon. The room was
gray and humid. And now she has passed away.

ii.

the remote

the mute

viii. [eating]

She realizes, *I love broth.* She especially loves the word *broth.* It sounds like *both.*

ix. [pretending to be ill]

She doesn't pretend to be ill because she fears bringing an illness upon herself. When young, she would locate stomachaches so she could stay home and compete with the baby for her mother. She would whimper and demand special food like ginger ale and rice gruel. Red Jell-O.

xi. ["new strategy"]

RE the novel: The woman was merely a suitable vehicle for his newfound fixation: the sand. Suna.

She could be the entomologist and the woman. She didn't have to choose.

xii. [things left]

Chicken defrosting . . . Computer on . . . Dry-cleaning ticket on the refrigerator . . . Bottle of Jack newly opened . . . Newspaper delivery . . .

xv.

In an old notebook: *My first boyfriend finally left me after so many arguments about not leaving. Love was not the issue: everything else was. What melodrama! I was left with the dog biting all the fur off her belly.*

She kept the apartment. He left with toothpaste, bottle of scotch, several clean shirts and jockey briefs. She packed all his other belongings in black garbage bags and they remained around her rooms for weeks. Like the body bags she grew up seeing on the 5 o'clock news, 1968.

xix. ["Repetition of the same patterns, they say, provides an effective form of protective coloring."]

xx. ["monotonous handiwork"]

xxii.

E-mail to her sister: *After he left, I mean after we separated, as I walked around the apartment or down the street, I'd talk to myself as if talking to him. Fortunately it was winter and my scarf covered my face.*

She called her sister to hear what her own voice sounded like. It was her protection though it also caused trouble at times.

But already she was not the girl full of regret.

xxx.

It was neither insects nor sand, but an odd devotion to devotion.

Wellfleet, Midsummer
(2000) continued—

24

The clumps of beached mussels squawk and whistle—but to what
end? It was a marriage frothy with grievances.

25

By my lover's rented cottage, a field of weeds that my father called
devil's paintbrush—in those days when there was still room for
him to paint.

26

Is the open area beyond the stand of pine—a meadow or marsh?
Will I *wonder* there without the man now sleeping beside me?

27

It is not the daughter's questions that disturb the morning air of
our rented beach cottage—but the tone. Crabs clambering out
of the mud as if to inspect. Or is it my ear?

31

It's a former life—the one bent over small children and a small dog,
tweezing ticks off all three. I think how I don't ever miss their
father.

32

A friend claims she grew up with fireflies on Fire Island but I've
never seen any—any wonder after years of fogging? Yet, mos-
quitoes gorged on the abandoning wife.

33

Loneliness is the habit of this house: even with two box turtles in a box on the porch I wonder what a home may be.

34

Standing on the deck with a cup of coffee, he sees a woodpecker he had not heard which I think we heard before waking. We recall things differently at times.

35

Do not compare *the long rains of my regret* with your flash flood of grief—I imagine saying.

38

How is that milkweed flower we saw before yesterday's downpour? Pity the classical poets who could not touch on such an exquisitely insignificant topic!

39

Should we hunt for moss this afternoon? And if we find any should we save it for my father's garden?

40

You close the bedside window this summer night—but I feel the draft even so. And it is not possible to draw you closer without suffering.

Sparrow

Bashō wrote: *The moon and sun are eternal travelers. Even the years wander on.* I always wonder about translations but can never recall enough Japanese to measure a text for myself. So many semesters of bungo and what I recall most is the plodding pace of those semesters in the wood-paneled libraries. Now I rely on translators and have collected five versions.

*

With small children the days pass achingly slow as one pulling her earlobe refuses to nap, the other refuses to sit still unless cartoons anesthetize; but the years speed past. Suddenly, it's true, the three-year-old is thirteen—taller than the mother and recalling the word *no* in numerous forms: *why should I? I'm going to anyway. Yeah, right.* Even retaining, *No, Mommy.*

Now, with children in this sublet, Saturdays though Tuesdays, I find time has changed. A lover on opposite nights. And the sorrow of flight as I continue to leave my husband; also the relief, not only of leaving our matched flaws, but from flight itself.

Who is the traveler but the heart—or, depending on the moment, the gut?

A flock, startled by a child's outburst, rises as a single lake of wings.

*

Of the five versions I've collected, one is entitled *The Narrow Road to the Interior.*

*

The dog slinks off my youngest daughter's bed when I enter her room to kiss her goodnight. It's our ritual: the dog hops up at her invitation, slinks off when I open the door, then hops up again when I leave. Flight also includes sleep as this child lies on her back, snores, then rolls over onto her side. Where is she? Only she knows and might not recall the journey upon waking.

Where was the adult before rising too late?

Then, too—legs on my lover's shoulders.

At this moment it is painful to leave and more painful to stay. Any residue of affection has twisted into an anger keen as a scalpel. Brilliant as a blade. Clean as glass. I wish to hold my husband, hold our *separating*.

> The body would like to recall humidity even
> or especially in February—
> even as the dogwood too early reddens
> then freezes the next week
> but is still not ruined.
> What of the nestled pupa, more
> uncompromising than we imagine?
> *

The brown branches, the pink moments.
I was *at a loss*.

Was marriage my imagination? I look at photos of cheery tanned profiles from little family vacations and cannot know what I was thinking.

*

As after my mother's death, I walk around seeing objects from a haunted world: a child's easter dress, box of four crystal glasses, unopened package of men's t-shirts. A beach towel. The delightful ones pin me to sorrow. *That bird.*

How to mourn someone who has not died? Although I know when a parent dies, the relationship still continues.

flocks

John says—about the lover's own ambivalence—*if the relationship weren't conflicted then you should worry.* What would I do without *him*?

      *

One morning my lover calls from a hotel bed one hundred miles away to say, *sometimes I feel complete relief for leaving her.* Or did he say, *grief?*

      *

I thought during my husband's long 10 p.m. walks that maybe he was purchasing sex in doorways then returning to refuse me. Or just sitting in the meridian hanging out with hookers then returning home to his own reticence.

When I finally told him *I'm leaving* he curled up in bed and heaved without noise. I grabbed the children and their jackets and pulled them into spring snow—to protect them from his grief? To protect myself? To keep them from both? To keep them to myself?

Is memory the same as recollection? As golden dancing slippers? As a sparrow's birthday cake?

His nightly walks paralleled my constant running off to one café or another, where I could reside safely for a couple hours. The comfort of hearing the clink of silverware washed in the kitchen, "Walk Away Renee" on Lite FM, someone cute attending the bottomless cup.

      *

Cid Corman and Kamaike Susumu translated those Bashō lines: *Moon and Sun are passing figures of countless generations, and years coming or going wanderers too.* And the version I used as a crib sheet in college, Dorothy Britton translated as: *The passing days and months are eternal travelers in time. The years that come and go are travelers too.*

Is memory really against travel—as it selects which interior?

*

In winter everything blackens,
the frozen ground turning its cold shoulder.
In this momentary return of mud
this or that man can exit
and the veins thaw
with the rise in temperature. How lovely
to anticipate the summer midafternoon
so humid it is difficult to breathe.
To then become that afternoon, now, if possible.

*

I make my home again and again: café on Sackett, café on
President, on 2nd Avenue waiting for John, on 99th waiting for the
girls to finish Japanese dance, on 52nd after breakfast with H, in
one hotel or other when traveling.

Or kneeling in front of him by the hall mirror, holding his ass. Or
his kneeling in front of me as I look in the hall mirror. Or bend
over the edge of the bed. Or perch on the desk, stockings off. Or
clothes half on, and half in a pile on the floor.

(Do the stacks of magazines, bills, children's toys, coffee cups—do all
these things drive me away even as I collect them to nest? *Yes*).

*

Were family vacations running away from home? *Yes.*

The mice burrowed in as soon as we closed the apartment door.

And what about this sublet of mine—neatly tended and straight-
ened each night when I tuck my daughters in, saying, *sticks-feathers-
string-mud—*

*

(The lover's *words* so unsettling they could override childbirth and ten anniversaries—so absolute, the words were not from his mouth but from an echo, a sounding.)

(Elizabeth Barrett Browning called it, *my childhood's faith.*)

*

    The more the petals blow off the more
    I find not grief but summer.
    Loss was before—as if in childhood seasons only.
    The winter cradled the seed, a wish
    for summer light flushing the colors out.
    Replying to others I forgot my self
    but returned with the vernal equinox. Yes?
    Yes, cherry, plum—
    yes, orchard of the aorta.
    The season's ruin, the heart's sigh.

Note to myself: jot down words like, *warming* and *warning. Cloister* and *cluster.*

*

That husband will always be the one who pulled the crowning infants—one daughter and the next. Who could not, as I could not, reflect more than one another's wounds.

Wound. Wind.

Wind.

*

Now time changes during flight—it pauses.

Roget's 3rd edition—under *verb*—"Cease to be." And I am startled and look up 2.5: "cease, . . . perish, expire, die; vanish, disappearing; . . . fade away or out, fly, dissolve . . . come to nothing." *Yes.*

(Legs straddling a vanity sink to wash before lovemaking. My powder and oils in the lover's medicine cabinet.)

*

Does the wren cry
when it cries into the graying air, confettied with seed?
A boy skips rope
on the pavement pink with torn blossoms. Then what?
Is the dragonfly afraid to love
what it may not understand?
The firefly? The firefly waits for
nightfall. Does he wait for nightfall?
She does. Though the females clustering together
may not wait at all.
Some may not even respond to light—I think.
But that is summer.
Could this be August?

*

Each *he,* first a vehicle for takeoff, then the impulse for the takeoff itself.

Okay.

*

But even humidity
is not a cure and warm rain
not a tonic
for bitterness: *look,*
I tell my daughters,
see how a magnifying glass
can light paper in the courtyard.
I linger there by the pink dogwood
now only a rustling green.
Does the courtyard matter?

*

I could not return to the body that contained only the literal world.

Where *sparrow* does not suggest *sorrow*.

Where *sorrow* does not suggest *sorry*.

Cranberry Island, Late Summer
(2000)

1

On waking, do I hear the waves first or smell the brine? And am I awake from my past marriage where dinner was a soundless downpour?

5

Fir trees volunteer among the stones above the beach. That was seeing him after I was resistless.

7

The water is probably not deep by the seaweed sloshing the rocks— but, like scorn for that former husband, who knows? Does he?

20

Our host knows where to rake for clams and where to pluck mussels for his estranged wife and friends. I think it makes him happy, a little.

9

Three of us clamming all morning with one hand rake, hands and knees smell briny well into the cocktail hour. How I love the word *ravish*.

11

Was it the clamming? After this trip we return to separate apartments with lumpy sofa beds. Knowing where what is, and, for now, with whom.

18

He squats in shallows to pluck mussels from a bed near his porch. I imagine cold. A touchy old woman will live in my home.

16

As a girl I thought the Milky Way was an evening cloud. Faint and frequent. Perhaps I needed it to be that close.

39

I didn't know if it was a loon. Is it female? Does another care? Do birds wonder?

22

I can't name the insect that clicks on the rocks beyond the stand of pine. Some things only my mother knew.

24

I've decided to climb the rocks beyond the stand of pine to find the insect that clicks like an old-fashioned toy.

26

But it's a grasshopper—black with yellow wings—making that clicking noise. My lover shows me he can name things before catching them.

41

This is where my wife wishes to be buried, a friend says in a pine grove. How lucky to know, I think to myself.

15

I can see him reading out on the porch, too gusty for my notebook.
I've searched for this man. Even my critical father thinks so.

36 for A.B.

As I hand him his mail, I cannot tell his age. Later I see why—this
island painter kayaks into the bay, barely distressing the water.

Gowanus, Late Summer
(2000)

2

The trees flinch in late summer air over Boerum Hill. We already
miss scorching on that Salt Marsh Road.

3

The summer was about rage. Will recollection fall dead off the trees?
Can it? I am the one who left.

4

Did my daughters hike to the Sunken Forest with their father this
summer? Is to imagine, to imagine regret?

5

When father took me fishing in a rowboat in the Catskills, a wall of
rain came over us. Were there cicadas?

14

No dejection on returning from this vacation—this man so deeply
attentive we might be lingering still, under the cicadas uproar.

9

If only I could know a plover—or warbler. But a suburban girl
learns little more than red and brown—or brown and brown.

8

Home from vacation, no fuzzy seeds soften the air. The former hus-
band's studied neglect has suddenly quit—is that it?

10

All the harsh remarks about him that he himself reported to me, I
now believe and repeat to those who made them. *Torrential.*

12

At any moment I can recall that downpour walking home from a
visit with my daughters—mostly the heart, the louder beating.

18

When the leaves shudder, despondent is the season. Soon I'll rise in
the window's dark light.

19

Isn't it true that the leaves on certain trees turn suddenly, before the
others? As suddenly, all the red is brittle. What if the lover
moves closer?

26

Thankful the former husband does not return in my sleep—*to my
dream pillow comes* the lover's plum preserves.

28

Will the Gowanus Canal look less leafy in the fall or more so—I do
not know since I've lived here so few seasons. Away from men.
With daughters.

29

The daughters' complaints escalate over anything. A breeze for
example. Happily the leaves scatter.

The Tunnel

responding to Kawabata Yasunari's *Yukiguni [Snow Country]*

First Snow: late December

The first snow reminded her of a cloud of insects swarming in August—of the days she would walk from the rented beach house to the little over priced grocery and walk into that swarm. They would stick to her eyes or she'd inhale a few into her nose. They were tiny as krill in a pail of seawater. They made her feel estranged.

She wanted to reread *Yukiguni* in the winter and see if what she had loved she still loved: the sharp almost surreal images laden with sentiment. The white. The passages.

I think so.

The snow was as deep as the startling white, and as her feelings for him. The snow burned her exposed fingers. The air burned her cheeks. There was no wind. The sun came and went. She knew she needed extravagant love affairs in order to feel this kind of scorch. And she was grateful this man did not interfere with her family life such as it was.

This is the room the silkworms used to live in. Are you surprised? (p. 53)

The geisha was independent because she could earn money—yet was bound by contract. And by a sorrow practically codified into an aesthetic. *Sabi*

Komako. What were the kanji? She would have to purchase a Japanese edition and dust off her Nelson's.

(And wasn't there a suffix indicating expectation? anxiety?)

But what can you say to a woman in broad daylight? (p. 26)

Is the translation, "is it" from *kashira*—I wonder.

I think so.

*

The bright snow the winter after Mother's death made her weep—
the glare itself. Weeping in the cold air hurt. And her mittens were
already so wet from the snow she couldn't wipe off her face.

Layers of clothes: two pairs of socks, silk leggings, pants, turtle-
necked shirt, flannel shirt, sweater, gloves, scarf, hat, down jacket.

This snow collected so quickly she wondered if she'd be able to
open the door in the morning. When would it stop?

He would not see her more than once a week. Never consecutive
nights. The snow evaporating on her sleeve was also ambiguous.

I think so.

Clumps of snow froze on bushes.

Snow so bright you could not look for long.

The snow that melted from the eaves pockmarked the snow around
his house.

*

After some ten years, she almost felt timid rereading the novel—
what if the story wasn't an appropriate gift? Would he understand
that more than the relationships, it was the imagery that had
moved her? Anyway, it was too late: she had already given him
the book.

He told her that he carried the book around with him although he
had not started it. They both knew he probably wouldn't. Not for a
long time after their affection had transformed into something else.
A passage.

A tunneling effect.

From her commute she knew that the subway tunnel was ahead.

(Her voice spiralled into the voice of a child when she called his apartment and his mother answered.)

It's no fun, though, swallowing sake down in the dark. (p. 146)

She, herself, wasn't in the mood for the leisurely pace—which made her feel listless. She did like Seidensticker's introduction: *The [haiku] manner is notable for its terseness and austerity, so that his novel must rather be like a series of brief flashes in a void.* (p. viii)

Maybe so.

What if—

Second Snow: early January

Her husband warned her not to stray and she wasn't. She was moving in that direction—she knew that, too, but would not betray his heart. At least. The snow outside was knee deep against their back door. She cracked the window and lay down. A ribbon of cold hit her face.

Hit her face.

After about a foot of snow on the first night of the blizzard, she trudged to the train to get to a benefit poetry reading. By the time she arrived she was so frozen that she drank a cup of real coffee and immediately began to shake. The snow that had stuck to her leggings melted and the wet chilled her all the more.

Did she like *Yukiguni* because of the triangle? Did it strike something satisfying? A loneliness? A dedication to escape to that?

She thought of the igloos she and May had made in her yard. Allowing her sister in. The color blue.

How being mean does not leave a mark. It leaves ambiguity. And terror.

Call you a geisha? (p. 20)

She didn't want to slip into lingerie for her husband, then, in his disinterest, feel stupid. Mostly, when rejected, she felt as if there were nothing inside her skin—no arteries, tissue, marrow. She wasn't sure how she could breathe.

*

The F train into Brooklyn was not running past the Carroll Street station—where the elevated rose above Red Hook's light industry and tenements, then returned to the tunnel.

No F train service to Manhattan.

I could not reach him.

Leafing through she finds there are compelling moments she had underlined when she was his age: *Her skin, suggesting the newness of a freshly peeled onion or perhaps a lily bulb, was flushed faintly, even to the throat. More than anything, it was clean.* (p. 73)

*

The second section was the novel she remembered—the insects' egg-laying season, the details of bleaching the Chijimi cloth on the snowfields. The tunnels beneath snow. The Milky Way, of course. Why did it feel different this time? Was it less white?

In her scribble *detail* resembled *derail.*

He warned her of his cruel streak. Saying things as if not knowing their effect. Adding her baby name, *Kimi,* as if to mask the cruelty.

41

Komako shook her head mildly and wiped at the table with her handkerchief.
"The place is alive with insects." A swarm of tiny winged insects fell from the
table to the floor. Several small moths were circling the light. (p. 95)

I recalled the bleached cloth but not the moths.

She recalled.

She wanted to wear a different kimono each day for him, so bor-
rowed from other geisha.

She was just forty.

*

What are the "themes": the white, or, more specifically dark on
white or white on dark, like Komako's powder, the loss of love, the
transience of it, the triangle men enter, the inability to love, the
coolness of heart, of rejection? How women treat women?

*

She wanted to catch up to his several drinks—knocked back a shot
of bourbon when they reached his apartment but by that time the
alcohol had run through his system and he was clear. Clear about
his desire and hers though hers was now something else. A flurry.

"Here in our mountains, the snow falls even on the maple leaves." She recited from
a Kabuki play. (p. 145)

At the sudden rise in temperature, the mounds of snow on the
street steamed like exhaust. Streams ran under them into the sewer.
Everything felt dirty but at least it was warm.

She recalled laying on her back in the snow fort, her back like ice,
and breathing in the icy air and breathing out the air warmed from
her own small body. She stayed until her mother called, *Kimi*, her
voice even more distant from outside the packed snow.

In her nostalgia she began watching Japanese soaps after the children went to bed. Understanding an occasional word—*kangae, tokorode, shiawase*—she felt pleased.

Abruptly, in the moth's egg-laying season, his wife figures prominently. Her admonition not to keep a set of clothes at the inn. The wife in Tokyo with their children. The egg-laying. The season. The screen on the window.

Maybe that's it.

It was only when her own daughter was born that her mother reappeared, as if from a tunnel. But that was no longer possible.

Brooklyn, Late Winter
(2001)

2

This is that time before summer when there is little to report:
  blossoms blown, leaves full blown, air not yet as blistering
  as leaving that husband's side.

6

Anyway—did Shikishi write on winter? did it suit her? Why should
  I? Why does the student write in such a way as to *not* express—

8

I need not write about those snow forts where I lay on my back
  looking up at the ceiling turning into twilight, my mother
  calling from the trite threshold.

Brooklyn, Early Summer

(2001)

18

On the answering machine, my daughter's voice reports *I'm not coming home*. At least she feels these close rooms are home—I whisper to the door.

20

They said it would drizzle. It showers—though we did not believe them. My lover did not.

21

She complains of sand in her two-piece. I tell her to bathe her sex in the surf. Away from the boys.

28

Rather than feel abandoned I ask for a glass of water. He brings a spare comforter.

30

Evenings before the fireflies hatch, I wish the season would hurry. And you, to my bed—if only to fall asleep watching a black-and-white movie.

34

I write more in spring. The window is open and the tumult, entirely familiar.

36

This summer noon: a daughter and her boombox in one room, a loud sparrow in the open.

38

Desperate, I focus my affection on the lavish summer leaves—as if
they will last and outlast.

40

Shallow of me—only noticing one bird this afternoon. Now I am sure
there were sparrows as well. I keep this a secret.

45

The morning glories twist shut in the late afternoon. Ah, closure is
that close!

48

When did we last identify three kinds of dragonflies? Was it before
you left your wife—or before I left my husband?

49

Really my seasons are defined by a single tree by the bodega across
the street. And the air. And the daughter's sharp curfew.

Pulse and Impulse

Black Twig, Rome, Fuji, Gala, Granny Smith, Macintosh, Red Delicious—
Sam, Sylvia, Nelson, Royal Anne—

January 1st. I was hoping to walk the dog in the Prospect Park meadow this
morning but the rain was coming down in sheets and she had to be dragged out
just to pee. Funny how much she dislikes rain and baths but so readily jumps
into messy puddles where possible. As long as it stinks.

Back home I'm reading Louise Glück's Meadowlands. What does that
phrase mean—to find words? "I'm sick of your world / that lets the outside dis-
guise the inside."

What does it mean for a woman to seeks models, whether as someone to
emulate or resist? And how is the body contained in one's work apart from sub-
ject matter?

I began with my own soft but tense body to seek words and a poetic—to seek
models who would guide. Mother was a model for the intuitive—which I didn't
understand or appreciate until I began to understand my own process—a process
of betrayal. The one I trust although I couldn't consciously comprehend her pow-
erful reliance on the unconscious. I don't believe she did either. That to some extent
it was cultural.

January 4th. Appointment with gynecologist this afternoon—PAP smear
positive. Which is a negative thing.

Emily Dickinson, Gertrude Stein, Edna St. Vincent Millay, Elizabeth Bishop,
Marianne Moore, H.D.—

I realize now that when Mother died in a car accident seven years ago—the
girls were four and six, I was thirty-eight—that I had never felt as deeply as when
I felt that loss. As though I'd never felt love or loss. And I began to understand
missing something I had always missed. Something my mother couldn't give me
because no mother can give a child what the mother gives in fairy tales. Which is
one thing she did give me—fairy tales. (Perhaps that is where girls learn about
the body: Sleeping Beauty, Rapunzel,—) Little did I know that my mother was
both the mother and stepmother in "Hansel and Gretel."

CJ tells me my inside and outside reside very closely. That is a good thing.

January 5th. I want to write poems that "answer" the quotes I garner from Louise's—even if completely out of context.

Murasaki Shikibu, Sei Shōnagon, Ono no Komachi, Lady Ise—

When deeply unhappy I lie down, cry, feel my whole body ripped open with sorrow. Delicious because it is delicious to realize feelings. As when Mother died I felt relieved to not feel numb but to lie down on the floor and weep.

So I began with my own soft but tense body to seek words and a poetic—a guide.

The mother and evil stepmother. I accept that.

Models? There's always the Japanese: Murasaki Shikibu's The Tale of Genji *and Sei Shōnagon's* The Pillow Book. *Both admired for their daring subject matter, aesthetics, and prose styles. I love Sei Shōnagon's "Sympathy is the Most Splendid of All Qualities." Also her list of "hateful things."*

I love the sense of abandon.

January 5th continued. *Why is it that the neighbors allow their dog and toddler to run in the common garden? I am not even sure which one is responsible for digging holes. In the spring we will see if any of the bulbs have survived their exuberance. I am glad to hear the delight but sorry to see even this muddy winter patch so worn. My annoyance sounds like the in-laws complaining that the girls always break something whenever we visit. Their busy little hands undoing or accidentally smashing this or that. Busy and delighted bodies in rooms meant for seated adults.*

The oldest is so full of her own delight—whether thumbing through catalogs for t-shirts and nail polishes or reporting some cliquish crime on the phone or writing an essay—that I sometimes forget how much she needs me. Her increasingly womanly body with a tiny child's face—needs me.

January 7th. *I am afraid to call the doctor. Finally afraid. Whenever I walk the dog I feel like I'm a little bit running away from home. The dog and leash are the tether.*

The threshold is not ambiguous there.

Shower, drizzle, mist, downpour, rain—

The winter is not ambiguous here.

Sam, Sylvia, Nelson, Royal Anne, Cashmere, Bing—

January 8th. *Classical Japanese was not my undoing but certainly caused further humiliation. I can still talk Japanese babytalk. I can still teach my daughters a few baby words or the words to cue them in Japanese dances: fune (boat), tegami (letter), naku (cry)—I can still feel the dances I learned in high school in my own limbs.*

(The folk dances are the same dances we perform in July for the Buddhist festival commemorating our ancestors. Now we dance them for her.)

With or without fluency, I can still love the zuihitsu as a kind of air current: and what arises is very subjective, intuitive and spontaneous—qualities I trust. Also a clear voice.

That it was cultivated by a woman and feels significant—as a writing space for women. It is by its own nature a fragmented anything. I love long erratic pieces into which I can thrash around—make a mess. Lose the intellect.

Begin with your own fleshy body to seek fragments that will sustain.

I think of what we are left of Sappho's work—so ravaged by patriarchal flames yet still enduring. Endearing.

I love Keene's phrase: "an intriguing sentence or two."

To invite the intellect back in for re-vision.

To feel randomness.

Not obliged to stay with a rational line of thought. I mean—I do not need to compromise a train of thought and, in such a way, can really explore raw material.

This "space" includes all those traits women have been assigned, usually with negative connotations: subjectivity, intuition, irrationality (what short essays or lack of a formal structure might suggest). What is wrong with subjectivity anyway? My facts. The fact of my experiences.

The doctor told me I need a cone biopsy and because I am not having any more children she will be "aggressive." I felt faint. I looked in her hands at the drawing of the uterus. I watched her point to the cervix and how she will cut.

January 9th. *I told a friend a few days later and she said she had a similar* procedure a year ago and had also been afraid. I asked her why she didn't tell me and she said because it's not something one talks about. Meaning: it's an ambiguous virus, sexually conveyed. I discovered a number of women who have not wanted to talk. Even the gynecologist does not know much—because it isn't something lethal to men perhaps there is little publicity—and a lot of shame.

There are areas of our life where ambiguity can be lethal. Where we explore intuitively.

Intuition, like subjectivity, is not treated as a valid, responsible trait.

Where to cut?

What makes sense? What is not fragmented? What is whole? Obviously if whole, the object embodies potential fragments. And in each fragment, the whole——which, speaking of poetics, we know from that impossible-to-pronounce figure of speech, synecdoche.

Where is ambiguity a pleasure and where does it censure?

(I do not mean to fetishize the fragment. Do not mean to suggest the woman's body should be so. I am afraid.)

Irrationality is not valued either. But when working with, for example, juxta-position, then the rational does not need to be sequential or to fit into a conventional framework. The "logic" of a piece may be closer to an "illogical" train of thought—for which of course many have been rewarded. But why not lose the mind—hold it at bay until re-vision.

Celebrate and bathe in these various air currents.

Miya, Rei, Kimi, Tomi—

Paragraphs absorb the emotionality differently than lineated poems. When I tried rendering a few scribbled paragraphs into conventional poems they did not work; there was an over-sentimentality that was not evident when in paragraphs. It wasn't that the feeling was camouflaged, more, there was an absorption, an acceptance of the emotion that the verse could not bear. ("Cuttings" stayed a zui-hitsu rather than a series of poems.)

Even the Japanese diary subverts the linear by including haiku.

It is lovely when a fragment can be a whole. Not just suggest entirety.

(Or can it?)

Where will she cut? And how much is aggressive?

January 11th. *Difficult to wait for results.*

Mother was so intuitive she seemed to disappear at times. As if thinking were less important than trains of thought. Sometimes that disappearing was a way to survive other people's needs, and I imagine, to locate her own self. I wish she could have been more present though. My need.

January 12th. *Somewhere there is a note on a Japanese aesthetic value called kaoru, fragrance. I have never been able to find the reference. Do I dare write to a former professor?*

The other ten-year-old girls on Reiko's basketball team are also energetic and unfocussed. It must be hormonal. They can barely stand still to listen to the coach. And are also entirely too polite. I'd like to see them get more aggressive with the ball. But when one does jump in the air to swish the ball—how stunning her body.

January 13th. *It's my first husband's birthday. Should I send a card? How young we were! How old now, this body that lifts free weights three times a week! This body I did not love till after I turned forty—and told myself whatever is flawed is a flaw—not an issue of, say, chocolate. What to tell my daughters?*

How can the body feel so healthy, look strong—and produce such alarming "tests"? The doctor will explore, cut away and scrape sections that look diseased.

How to expose what lies hidden? To publish?

Red, Green, Iceberg—

Musk, Sweet, Winter, Wax, Yellow Doll, Honeydew—

January 15th. *I know that male philosophers have omitted the body, impure flesh, from their philosophical work on soul, morality, ethics, etc. That women philosophers have begun to insist on the body.*

Not just the outside or inside.

January 19th. *The youngest doesn't want me to go on a book tour. I gave her a notebook to write to me everyday and report what she's done. We held one another. She calmed down.*

Great Barrington, Spring to Summer
(2001)

1

I cannot wait to stay with you on that lawn without shadows. But
what of my children, their belongings?

2

In the sunny meadow without dew, the thrush calls, *What?* Though
the mockingbird recalls: *Why?*

3

In the meadow without mist one bird calls and a different kind
recalls. I am sorry. Full of sorry.

10

A crow disrupts the shadow of the leafy bush by the borrowed
house. There are no berries. No gnats. No homesick.

13

A butterfly in the milkweed. A bat whisking the pond. Sweet
dreams, my beloved.

14

We plot against mildew and I think of Father who no longer distin-
guishes between journals and the scent my daughters call
grandpa's house.

15

The bees are always eating. Or if they do something else I don't
notice. Like when the children were small.

16

On my wet morning jog, I see seven birds, each bright as a
    postcard; yesterday, two somber egrets. Tomorrow? One
    regret?

18

For myself, these pressed meadow blossoms, if only to recall the
    names Mother taught us girls. Will I?

19

Yesterday a field of rain. Today, a field of mist.

28

How did it come to this: a mother separated from two daughters
    three nights a week? Do they miss the dried flowers I taught
    them to arrange? Taught that scent *is* memory.

29

All summer my daughters stay out late so I see them less and less—
    but hold them more, it seems.

31

The forecast promises a drop in temperature but it was just a
    prediction. Why should his heat break?

32

What about his stay? What about the rain? And his fog?

34

Will he stay? The trees thrash in this storm and abandon the
blossoms. Leaves will follow.

38

When I see my daughter, my sorry heart is fuller than a storm
cloud. It is midsummer and filled with ozone.

39

Shallow of me to wonder if my daughter thinks me heartless. She
alone resides with her father's grief this late summer.

44

The daughter phones from camp where calls are not permitted. She
calls because I miss her.

45

By accident I smash a tiny spider in the bathroom. What was that
warning?

46

All morning I think of a tugboat on the Hudson. Red. That red.
I miss my daughters that much more.

47

Soon the pear in the orchard will fall and rot. Then take root. What
nature teaches us about mothers every day.

Blunt Instrument

11.30

Scratch the surface, uncover rage. A new emotion, not unlike a toy–
–although not always a pleasure. I feel differently in control: rather
than a candied comment, I hear myself saying *ohfuckoff* and am
amazed. I once confined this stuff to metaphor. Aimed for a volatile
tension in each line. How satisfying to read aloud those poems
about cutting him off at the knees. At once dismembering the man–
–*and* safeguarding the children's father.

      *

www.anthro@veracity.org
And at least one version must come from an old woman.

TO: johnw@queens.edu
I love how Japanese regard veracity: from *Japanese Poetic Diaries*, Earl
Miner comments: "Bashō is shown to have fictionalized, altered, and
later revised [*The Narrow Road Through the Provinces*]." Also, "[in Japanese
diary literature] there is an artistic reconstitution of fact participating
in or paralleling fiction." And on my favorite *nikki*: "the Japanese
transition from fact to art is of course in the diary rather than the
letter, and it is made very explicitly in the first sentence of *The Tosa
Diary* [by Ki no Tsurayuki] . . . because the author is a man using
the narrative point of view of a woman." Hardly the Western tactic.

"This pose [as a woman] was remarkably prescient [because of the
coming domination of women in literature]." (*ibid.*)

      *

Monday—a sparkling blue morning. The children at day camp.

Monday—a cool dark morning—the mist rolling up the beach. The
children still asleep.

Monday—a rainy afternoon. The children overdosing on tv.

It was a Sunday—I circled classified ads in the real estate section—
imagined leaving his shit for good. Who knows where the children
were.

*

12.1

Even though I am the one who left the marriage, now that he is
seeing someone (a trust-fund divorcée!) I am livid with resentment.
Why did I stay all those years! If I could beat him to a bloody mass
I would gladly collect blunt instruments.

. . . collect anything sharp.

. . . collect household poisons.

*

TO: harolds@mindset.com
Confessionalism in poetry? I'm not clear why this issue has come
up since I've always assumed poetic license—so any "confession" is
bound to be fictive.

12.2

The student insists on telling the truth, even *boring* truth. (Actually
boring would be great if in the sense of *drilling*.)

12.2

The daughter, in writing about betrayal is writing about *herself* for a
change.

www.anthro@veracity.org
And at least one telling must issue from an older woman.

*

12.2 continued

My students mistake blurting something out for poetry. Nerve replaces craft.

. . . collect fluffy pillows.

FM: harolds@mindset.com
Was it Picasso who said, "Art is the lie that tells the truth"? I think so but better look it up if you're going to use it.

FM: johnw@queens.edu
Who suggested that lyric poetry is somehow truer than narrative? I can't recall where I read that—*The Kenyon Review?*

    *

12.4

I told him that I really hate how joking was a means of humiliation. One where the recipient is asked to participate. That I would go sit on the toilet in the dark. I thought he was asleep but he was awake. *He knew.*

12.4 continued

I'm reading an antique handbook on autopsy. The diction from a vivisection text is so pure.

[What his best friend told me he said]
She thinks I found pleasure but I was as present as I was able.

    *

12.5

He knew he recalled my mother's rejection.

Like his mother.

Like my mother.

Yours.

www.anthro@veracity.org
From a woman with silver hair.

*

Q: How autobiographical is your last book?
A: I never admit to sexual intercourse with X.
Q: So it is not important?
A: The poems convey the illicit—although in revision I struck out
  obvious references. Because of my daughters. It's wrong. Or at
  least cowardly. Or maybe *implying* is more *artistic*? I could think
  that and feel righteous.
Q: Is the real question—effect?
A: Effect or affect?

Notes for ENG 395 (Comp Lit): "But if Issa's intention [in *Oraga
Haru*] is not purely autobiographical, and we find that his account
of what purports to be a 'historical' year is actually an artistic
deception, and that he has woven into the fabric suggestions and
experiences which come from other years and other areas of his life
and mind—if indeed some of them be not pure fiction. He has, with
the instinct of the real artist, shaped this year so that it may more
fitly reveal the truth of him as a man than any one year, historically
considered, could possibly do." [from the intro. by Nobuyuki Yuasa]

*

TO: johnw@queens.edu
Do I mute my material instead of holding onto details that hit a
nerve? To protect others? And then feel furious? Do men do the
same? Sometimes I feel I need two separate writing lives: one that is

risky but edited—the published version; the other, one to be kept in
that proverbial secret chamber. Maybe to be published, maybe not.
In fact I do have a secret sheaf I keep in my desk at school. I feel
nauseous admitting this.
REPLY:
Save the rough drafts.

. . . collect fluffy pillows.

＊

TO: johnw@queens.edu
And what about his penchant for the Other—though this one looks
like family.
REPLY:
You're suggesting?
REPLY:
That he was raised to view the body as something not to be soiled;
that he chooses someone who does not resemble the mother—
because it's all right to soil the Other.
REPLY:
What is more interesting to me is how all your complaining about
your ex, how all the supposed-confessional stuff—really goes from
complaining to becoming *his* biography. It is really not about you.
He's become the subject. How funny: you've allowed the man to
become the subject. Again.

＊

[What his best friend told me he said]
I fell in love with her because she made herself so vulnerable.

＊

She suggested a good old-fashioned lead pipe.

She suggested rat poison.

She suggested anything from the kitchen.

Q: Does it really matter?
A: Because no one reads poetry?

The student typed *farther* instead of *father*. Another, *pubic* instead of *public*. *Voracious* instead of *veracious*.

jesuschristsowhat

    *

[I tell my best friend what I said to him]
Quit telling my father about your sex life with your loser girlfriend because I end up hearing about it—and the fact is it's pathetic. The fact is, in our marriage, you barely scratched the surface—it was my responsibility to say something? I did. You couldn't hear me, you were so busy licking your psychic wounds. You fuck.

[What his best friend told me he said]
I've told that bitch a million times I did the best I could. I did not find pleasure in hurting her—I did feel good shutting her up in that argument towards the end when she was provoking me—suggesting we try to be as intimate off our one vacation as we can be on. It felt good to shout—to be in control.

    *

    12.8

Adam Phillips: "For Freud the first question—the unconscious question—is, What do I want? and then, What fantasies of truth do I need to legitimize it?"

to beat him unconscious.

to tap the unconscious.

    *

TO: johnw@queens.edu

Is this just more pomo-self-indulgence? An excuse not to master (uh—) scansion?
REPLY:
More! More! More of everything!

    *

Q: Pillows?
A: The truth, even in the elegies, is fueled by rage.

Beat, thrash, flog, pummel, lash, club—

Blow, stroke, hit, knock, rap, pound, whack, punch, dash, sock—

Kick, jab, ram, strike, hammer, batter, slap, club, boot, stamp—

12.10

I bought a hammer when I moved into this apartment—a small one. I noticed it's labeled, a *woman's hammer*.

    *

Slay, exterminate, eradicate, dispose of, destroy, slaughter, butcher, strangle, decimate—

    *

12.11

Vivisection is not practical. I am not interested in the careful slice. The tender attention. What I want is gore. All over. And adrenaline. A chronicle of my rage.

    *

Who said?

Brooklyn
November 11, 2000

Wellfleet, Late Summer

(2001)

2

By the outdoor shower, the pine drop their needles in the sandy
   soil. By morning we find them in our double bed.

5

Rain a third day. We'll still walk at low tide to look for moving
   things. I can stop thinking about my daughter for a second.

9

When he picks a conch out of the bay it furls back inside. Who
   wouldn't?

17

Rolls of waves off Wellfleet. This could be Maui. I could be my
   mother.

19

At the beach I avoid the blankets of squalling children but miss my
   own.

25

Lying together on a towel, the sand flies bite us till we return to the
   rented bungalow. What strange foreplay!

33

Returning with bagels and the news, a cicada has fastened onto the
   screen door—a broach for a daughter I think I don't think
   enough of.

34

About boys' hearts her daughter does not know; but at the ozone
    before a storm she closes the window halfway.

35

About her daughter's whereabouts she knows enough; but of
    dragonflies, she collects books.

36

About ocean currents I do not know; but of the gulf in this
    daughter's heart, I can well recall my own.

37

About his past marriages I do not wish to hear; about what he
    finds at low tide, we will consume.

39

The sharp sunny day turns to midday haze; I weep *for no reason at all.*

8

I stop by Sam's Clam Shack because I'd seen dried silver dollars
    and imagined Mother pulling over. I break off a stalk though
    she died eight years ago.

44

I teach my daughters and his to rub the dried sheafs off silver
    dollar stalks: one of the few things my mother thought to
    teach me. And it does prove useful.

Boerum Hill, Late Summer
(2001)

43

I miss most the outdoor shower. Nine at night. A light rain over the
spray. A light from the bedroom window where he reads about
psychopathology.

42

I would cut and carry home all the weeds along the Gowanus
Canal—if the guys from the cement factory weren't watching
me over their thick sandwiches.

45

Even in Brooklyn we hear cicadas—whose young suck the roots of
trees for seventeen years. No curfew. And no disputes.

The Orient

Inside, the radio rides from "I Walk the Line" to "Big Yellow Taxi." Because the door is open, the outside traffic rhythmically blurs each song. I sit in my aerobics leggings and tee waiting for a cup of coffee and buttered bagel. The *girl* behind the counter switches up to The Temptations.

Your husband called here Monday—looking for you, she says loudly in my direction. She smiles. The air is sweet with women—even the men who wander in to order tea or shoot pool are this kind of sweet. And it doesn't have to do with *orientation.* The barkeeper knows I'm married to a man but suspects I may be more than a patron or tourist.

*

ORIENTATION: to be located or placed in a particular relation to the points of the compass; to be familiar with or adjusted to a situation—

"The *Orient,*" according to Said, is not only adjacent to Europe and one of its richest colonies but also is "its cultural contestant, and one of its deepest and most recurring images of the Other."

This is where I write.

This is where I write zuihitsu—for the permission, the blur, the rooms created by the little blocks of text.

Not unlike Duras or Wittig, I think to myself. Or *Paterson.*

This is where I write almost everything—at a little café on 5th Avenue in Brooklyn. A small table just out of the sun. *Hey girl. Hey Kimiko. Hey. Mornin'.* They blast the music. Joan Armatrading maybe. Salsa at times. Other times a radio channel.

Turn the channel.

Static.

She's losing the frequency. *Turn the channel*, someone suggests.

Said, going further in his introduction writes: "the Orient has helped to define Europe (or the West) as its contrasting image, idea, personality, experience."

*

Switch the station.

I am the only Asian-looking *girl* here. From my bookbag I pull out Ki no Tsurayuki's *Tosa Diary* where he writes in the voice of a woman who has lost a child. Writes in a *woman's-hand* to permit greater emotional license, the men of the tenth century too restricted by their own conventions. They needed the women for an expansion of form and content. They needed the women in order to use a new language. They needed difference.

*

An old boyfriend meets me for coffee and kisses me on the cheek. The barkeeper eyes us and scowls. I am embarrassed. Her name is Cicely.

I dream about her I am so embarrassed. Or *something.*

Is it the channel?

What's at stake?

*

The zuihitsu, spatial in every way, differs from the nikki, a "poetic diary" which differs from the Western—that is, differs from documenting fact unless we mean an emotional fact. Differs from what is really *true.*

Translated as *running brush*, I love the way the zuihitsu runs with the content.

But even with a hint of narrative, the form also relies on sensibility and spatiality—and a way to identify with the most important writers in the world, who happened to be Japanese women. I love them.

Like some teas? she asks. *Or drinking your usual?* I smile and reply, *the usual—but I do like the tease.* She grins back.

I love the unabashed first person—it almost risks the confessional quality that a diary exudes, or that diary-like information can contain in a conventional poetic form. Even the tone becomes altered by the form.

(What *is* true *here?*)

      *

I return home after rewriting a short story. Peel off a sweaty unitard. Shower and slip on a velvet skirt and loose cotton top. I sit at my computer to see where the words have taken the heart. The brain enters now.

      *

From Ki no Tsurayuki we know that *kokoro* and *kotoba* combine as the basic dynamic in Japanese poetics: the heart and the words produce passion, even if subtly placed.

      *

On my way to Harvey's book party I stop by the café for a takeout decaf. *It's evening,* Cicely remarks from a table of girls where she's hanging now, off hours. *You're confusing me,* she continues. I smile and reply, *Sweet.*

From confusion to clarity. From clarity to ambiguities, blurs, fuzziness. Haze.

In her *Gender Trouble*, Judith Butler asks, *How does language construct the categories of sex? Does "the feminine" resist representation within language? Within a language of presumptive heterosexuality, what sorts of continuities are assumed to exist among sex, gender, and desire? Are these terms discrete?*

construct
constrict

I am wired from Cicely's caffeine-mixed decaf.

Otherwise—what?

　　　＊

Maybe I am attracted to this *elegant mongrel* because it blurs categories: those "grade B" forms of the Western canon: letters, diaries— even gossip. Plus lists, fiction, criticism, online sites. I love blurs. I appreciate categories but as I grow older, have less of a need for the absolutes I sought in my twenties. The form suits this desire to blur.

She asks what I'd like. I ask for more caffeine. To wire the whole room.

Let me get something straight: I love cocks and often the men to whom they're attached; and I've never even slow-danced with a woman. But I'm increasingly drawn.

the pulse—

the impulse—

The impulse is to categorize: bi, lesbian-wannabe, a gay man in a straight woman's body, queer but straight—

Maybe she thought that ex-boyfriend was a girl? Or a gay man? Is he?

　　　＊

Curious how crazy straight guys are about lesbians—as if women's sex and sexuality are destined to be about the male. For me there's no quiver in seeing a gay porno flick. It isn't about *my* desire.

And this isn't about *coming out*. But emotional truths.

        *

I know there are times when I feel boyish: regulation push-ups (fifty), chinos and boots, JD (my dad's preferred drink—one of the few things we have in common)—

Maybe Cicely is thinking to tell me, *Easy for you girl—you can imagine, you can play, you can return home to the husband. The safe, straight life. Right?*

To the female sensibility: lipstick, gauzy clothes, . . .

(Can we allow ourselves to *feel what we want?*)

(The gendered feelings fit into cultural categories—it's true, but like the zuihitsu, they may appear splintered to a Westerner—which I am. I would prefer—prefer?—rejecting particular categories. Would she say, *Easy for you to say—from your privileged position.* I have come to realize what I desire is not so much to make love to a woman but to be deeply and openly intimate in a way that is as physical as my already emotionally open intimacy. Is this "queer"?)

        *

"Drawn"?

"Drawn and quartered"?

        *

Did you think this would be about ethnicity? *That* blur?

(Artists can weave in and out of categories like class—though I always forget which fork to use first. When to slip on one's elbow-length gloves. I am partisan but get off on bourgeois niceties. Benefit from them.)

I love words that confuse—

—how words can arouse. So the words are mine. The lover is mine. The lover's attention is mine. I am powerful. The lover is powerful. The words themselves.

Mine—the noun and verb. *That* blur.

The blur where the skin feels prickly. Pleased and desirous. *Delirious.*

     *

Is there a place in the English language for women? Yes and no. Yes, because women teach children language—even at this end of the century. And no, because men still own the means of production. But because culture is so incredibly susceptible to change the more women publicly use and abuse words—and its very syntax—the more women revise it in their own image.

Construct. Construe.

Perhaps diaries and letters are too feminine or female to become *canon* fodder.

In publication women come very close to owning their words though in that instant it becomes both the property of the capitalist *and* available within the market.

canon
cannon

cannot

I tell several female friends about this piece and only one does not change the subject.

   *

I would love to have a drink with k.d. lang. Wouldn't you? Which outfit would she wear? Suede jacket and cowboy hat? Which would I wear? What would I drink? (*Jack*—remember?)

Change the subject. Change the frequency.

Change the static.

What does become clear through the blurring is the experience of blurring itself.

Do I know how to slow-dance with a woman? Who would lead?

Boerum Hill, September
(2001)

1

Overtaking the crisp air, from across the Bay, blow pages of documents and ashes of terror.

2

The haze on an otherwise clear day reminds us of terror—won't allow even a daydream to swerve my mind away from the collapse.

3

A neighbor hoses down her small front garden: snap peas, zinnias, morning glory vines, grief. So much grief.

5

Trying to make a daughter's lunch. Trying to find the other's transit pass. Trying to find a moment to collapse.

6

More terror? Across the street this time? At a midnight clap of lightning, I sit bolt upright—

7

Firefighters scribble their names and social security numbers on their arms before digging into the rubble for their comrades. Digging into ash for a pulse.

13

Where once I sold silk ties to brokers, now the floor is a makeshift
  morgue lined with the burnt and shattered. This is as far as I
  allow imagination.

12

Once an afternoon for groceries, it is still an afternoon for groceries—
  and a fear once called *the bridge, the stray suitcase, the rental truck
  parked too long on the corner.*

8

From the Promenade—where my daughter and I saw Tower Two
  collapse—we look for something more than disbelief.

15

Taped to every lamppost on every corner are missing-person
  photos of the dead—6,965 to date. And after a thunder shower,
  fresh flyers appear as if from nowhere.

14

Day eleven: after days of sun and two of rain, the soles of the
  rescue workers' boots melt on the still-feverish metal wreckage.

Trading Words

But mere words were inadequate vessels to contain
the sense of shock and horror that people felt.
R. W. Apple, *The New York Times*, 9.12.01

falling bodies

falling bodies

and—*blind skyscrapers*

9.11

This morning, sitting in our little kitchen, glossed yellow by the clear
sunny day, I heard something like a single crack of thunder. Less
than a hour later—T called to tell me *a plane crashed into the World
Trade Center* and M and I ran to our Brooklyn side of the harbor.
There, we saw smoke billowing out of two monstrous holes in the
Towers—by *monstrous* I mean several stories high. Then the collapse.
Then smoke in our faces. *Two planes. Smoke.*

9.12

The conflagration was a spectacle, not unlike an Imax screen where
fire sparks just beyond fingertips. Then, when I began to hear
reports of casualties, my gut began to twist up. When M wanted to
visit friends—in the guise of "getting farther away from the harbor"—
and I wanted her to stay indoors with me, our argument became
ugly. T drove over to pick her up. It is a pattern we are trying to
avoid; one parent bailing out the other by whisking off an angry
child. The mundane cracks through crisis.

collapse

9.13

A photo of a dozen people standing on ledges of windows never meant to be jacked open. A photo of people emerging from a tunnel of smoke. A photo of dozens of shoes. No one has claimed responsibility.

9.14

Poems circulating online. Especially Auden's "September 1, 1939." Uncanny phrases replay in my mind: **blind skyscrapers—**

bridges and tunnels

blood banks

9.15

The unmentionable odour of death / Offends the September night.

9.16

Calls from across the country. Telling—who has *not* called. Meanwhile, when we ordered gas masks 24 hours after the attack, the prices had doubled from $20 to $40. Now they're up to $150.

white powder

smallpox

sleepers

9.17

Trouble sleeping—and when I do, I wake and cannot fall back because I'm convinced I should send the children to relatives outside the City. Then I think—but they should stay *with me.* Then—but not if their safety is in jeopardy. The conflict is constant. In this attack—there is no one field or beachhead.

sleepers

cells

9.18

The horror blurs my once-strict politics. Blur. Haze. Fever. How to defend ourselves and *not* plunge into war? Would silence or inaction be a defense of, say—stoning women? Of not permitting women to walk down the street unescorted, without a veil—even to beg for food? *There is no such thing as the State / And no one exists alone.* Of executing adulteresses, amputating a thief's hand, denying a girl's education, denying a woman's medical care?

9.19

We have our own sick fundamentalists: *The abortionists have got to bear some burden for this because God will not be mocked.* Rev. Jerry Falwell.

9.20

I have mixed feelings about the Auden poem. Moved by its cadence—its grace—and the passionately elegant images—well, I guess I don't have mixed feelings. I distrusted the *we* at first: ***We must love one another or die.*** I favor this tone: ***Our world in stupor lies.*** The meter. Diction. Was my crankiness really that critical reader who always steps critique-first? What an awful way to live. . . . Meanwhile, my own poems are rubbing up against sentimentality.

9.22

There's little else to talk about: bioterrorism or what to cook for dinner.

radius

9.25

I've printed little cards with emergency instructions for the girls to carry. Everyone says it's only a matter of time before the next attack. What to do—besides pack a flashlight, bottle of water, handkerchief to cover one's face in the event of biological attack. *A biological attack?* I think of a puppy whose guts exploded after eating rat poison.

9.30

Reports continue—of smoke, heat and darkness. A chaos of command. Report from a paramedic—it smelled like a butcher's. From a secretary, of being swallowed up by dust and fire. From a niece, who saw bodies falling outside her window. From a firefighter, who called his wife to say good-bye before entering the Tower.

10.11

All I have is a voice / To undo the folded lie . . .

10.12

What has happened to words?

10.15

How to prevent plunging into *war?* *That* wordlessness—

B-O-A-T

In the little rowboat at Lake Sebago my father and I could see the rain as a sparkling wall heading towards us from the green-black mountain. He told me to take my shirt off and stuff it under the seat. We reeled in our lines. I don't recall the downpour, only my dry top—was it Dotted Swiss?—and being with my father, apart from my mother and baby sister who were both in the cabin napping. Was I seven? And along the walk home, the black snake across the path.

I've always wanted to travel in a glass-bottom boat! To rub my feet on the glass and watch the deep—a dream one wakes from then wishes to will back in sleep.

He said in the navy they'd tie their whites to a line and drag it in the wake at high speed then hang them up—the salt, a natural starch. It pleased him to tell me that anecdote—also chewing ginger for bellyaches and going AWOL to visit a local museum.

He said—a different he, not my father—*in those days if you were a gay sailor you just shut up about it dammit.* Then, *why do those gays make such a big deal about sex?*

   *

Notes:

I am looking through my work for moments of boats. *As proof.*

   *

  . . . In his boat
the lap of the waves against the hold
was too intimate as he leaned back to sleep.

   *

At Noah's Ark Nursery School—which I called nose-ark—in back of the Lutheran Church of Our Redeemer, we had a rowboat filled with sand for a sandbox. I tell my lover my time with him reminds me of that pleasure—sitting on that little seat. That he is a lifeboat.

—my dream boat—oh, yeah

In a favorite photo of my mother she is wearing striped pedal pushers and reclining in a lounge chair, holding me in a blanket in her arms. The sun warms her face and sea spray is suggested by the other glistening chairs on the deck of the U.S. Something.

    *

Before he left the hospital and its "intensive care unit"
he asked me to write a poem for him.
It is a waka.
But I want to write another one
with the central metaphor, a boat.

    *

    WAVE
    FIN
    BOAT

    *

In 1972 when I told my father *if girls are drafted, I'll dodge,* he replied, *you'll join the navy like I did.* Shocking from a man who'd traveled to Dr. King's "I Have a Dream" March years earlier. Shocking to hear this in response to seeking his approval, for once.

    *

I copied poems from The Orchid Boat *for X.*

    *

As proof of boats!

The little ferryboat was a time capsule between the sizzling parking lot and swimming, although the beaches were exclusively visited by white people. A friend remarked upon vacationing there—*my god you must have been a freak!*

My daughters were too young to consciously understand the

racism of the summer community and cried on the ferry going home, their wet faces sprayed by the waves as the captain sped on to his destination. The crabcakes in the little stand by the dock cheered everyone up for different reasons.

I am determined to read past the Cetology chapter!

*

After reading my book she wanted to show me her own passion and took me on a sailing race—unfortunately it was a cold June afternoon and I sat in the noxious hold most of the three hours, frozen and green. But I didn't throw up.

Why would this Portuguese sailor come over to me and in his broken English point to the tattoo of a geisha as if I would identify with it. And I did a little. And why would he expect to get me into his boat.

I desperately wanted to see a whale breach—and we boarded a boat in Provincetown (Jeanne—were you strolling down the dock to Mark's?). While I did see several pods I was mostly in the bathroom or shivering in my lover's arms—green green green!

*

Grandpa took me fishing for sunnies. The lake was a tiny round mirror, like memory itself.

The text most frequently referred to is Ki no Tsurayuki's *Tosa nikki* where he writes in the persona of a mother traveling by boat to the capital, leaving behind the province where her little daughter had just died. She lies down on the floor and cries aloud. *He does.*

I finally get my wish: to ride in a glass-bottom boat—and on the world's second largest underground lake. Hiking into the Tennessee Sweetwater cavern, we find ourselves at the lip of the water. A shivering young man is waiting at the helm and all us tourists climb in.

Lights brighten the milky water and through the glass we see
dozens of shadowy trout swim up for the chum he's tossing over-
board. I was right—it could be a dream!

      *

Back then my boyfriend and I would sit in our borrowed car on
the ferry and try to stay warm though it was midsummer and visit-
ing his elderly aunt was our one vacation. How we loved to go
clamming by the dock!

Sometimes I would buy a hotdog then eat it on a bench. The Staten
Island Ferry was just a dime and we'd ride it just for the cheap
breeze.

Starting a Zuihitsu on *Eyebrows* and Discovering *Cocoon*

Her sister had begun to pluck all her eyebrows off and repaint them in orange arcs. Orange lipstick to match. They frightened her.

nymphs

caterpillars

There is a Japanese tale of a girl renown for her rebellious nature. She collected insects, play-fought with neighbor boys, and would not pluck her eyebrows in the ladylike manner of the time. Of course her father, rich though he was, began to have difficulty countering her reputation. Their servants believed, just by looking at her caterpillar-eyebrows, that she was ill fated. But this was not to be so.

On the E: *Yeah. Cost only ten. And he does great—look—just starts from the back. Plus—cheapa than LONG-GUY-LAND. Ya know?*

mayu

Even in her placid state she could see the endodontist's eyebrows above his surgical mask. Despite the anesthetic, her mouth was throbbing. Despite the throbbing, she was curious.

root canal on Utopia Pkwy

eyebrow-threading in Flushing

She was destined for, not *difficulty,* but for a man who truly cherished eccentricity. The caterpillar girl. He courted her with a lacquer container of cocoons.

mulberry

pluck

She had pluck, all right.

When I look up *eyebrow* in my dusty English-Japanese dictionary, I find the entry below, a homonym, is *cocoon*! I had first looked up *mayumi* but that means *spindle tree*.

The radical for *eye*—makes me long for Japanese. For Mother.

[CHIEN 3 * I: grass/leaves 1–3 are eaten by grubs 13–18 to make silk thread 7–12 for cloth 4–6 (= R cloth)]

knitting eyebrows

the endodontist's curly eyebrows

So she married after all.

A teengirl blog warns her readers not to pluck little "sperm-shaped" brows! Imagine!

Boerum Hill, March
(2002)

15

At night, the tip of Manhattan offers a lavish glow—if only it weren't
from the 24-hour recovery team.

16

Fathers and brothers who in a day's work fight fires—will not give
up searching in the subzero wind for remains.

17

Soldiers in green-camo appear at the mouth of each tunnel. Is this
autumn?

18

Nearly five months later: burying their lost husbands, some widows
carry their newborns.

19

"Her husband's remains"—as tentative buds appear this March,
what does that even mean, "remains"?

20

Five months after losing her husband, she buries him: at least the
hard earth softens.

21

Fathers and brothers sift dust in Fresh Kills—even on a subzero
morning—for any remains. Here in Brooklyn, spring arrives:
dutch elm, dogwood, cherry. Immeasurably.

22

Perhaps we could call these tourists, queuing up in subzero weather,
mourners. Though they bear cameras and camcorders.

25

The beams of light memorializing the dead in this spring mist are
not a tourist attraction. Please. We see them every clear evening
in Boerum Hill.

Firsts in No Particular Order

Purple towel on Grove, down comforter on South Davenport, deck
in Lonelyville, then of course—that rug burn, outer borough—

A Buddhist Temple storage closet over the humid dōjō—

My mother in a pine coffin on a late morning in early March
before they slid her body into the furnace for all time—

"Ruby Tuesday" on the car radio before the caesarean; "Louie Louie,"
before the vaginal—

Water radicals—

Grandpa's teeth in a glass and *shame shame for laughing*—

White moiré taffeta. Snow. *Blondie*—

Pinky

Air Pocket

The Waldorf-Astoria—

Olivetti Lettera 22—

Dialectical historical materialism, lumpen proletariat, dictatorship of
the proletariat, moribund capitalism—

Levine's "Gin"

Keep her cool. It's a febrile seizure. Not uncommon.

Chlorine

The lights opened on my powdered-white face, tiny red lips and
skeins of pink silk—a dance my daughters will dance—

K - I - M   M - O - M

Eight hundred quarters—

My mother, my mother—

Rowing with Daddy in the Catskills even while it poured—

Martini up with olives—*was it stirred?*

Things That Make Me Cry Instantly—

a baby crying in a diner booth—

the final paragraph of the child's story where the father and little girl turn home having finally spied a great owl, pumping its great wings in the brilliant moonlight—that book—

giraffe—

your gravity on mine—your sweaty pulsing inside me, your beard chafing, your lips on mine telling me in an artificial respiration how dear I am—that weight—

the thought of the word, *train*—

my two daughters dancing *momijinohana*, the drums' slow beat, the turning around to face the backdrop then the audience again—

even as the youngest drops her fan, giggles till she shakes but continues, that—my body quakes because my mother is dead and she watched me dance this dance in her peach-colored kimono in 1968. Yes, it was that long ago.

Things That Are Full of Pleasure—

Finally I have a dress that resembles my mother's except for the buttons. It is a lamby dress: grayish white and furry like wool. A waist. Three buttons down the front, mine in red, and hers—black with red in each center. She has tied a red ribbon around my ponytail also. I love her. I love that we look the same. Am I four?

My grandfather in Wisconsin teaches me how to dog-paddle. The bottom of the lake is soft.

pine, leaves, rose, hedges, stem

Dad shows me how to wind wire around tiny pine tree branches. It is five years old but only a few inches tall. We collect new moss to cover the roots.

The smell of hibiscus. Gardenia. I think of my grandmother.

I think of mango trees.

My first husband speaking street Spanish.

My second husband taking my hand and guiding me out of the rough waves I had gotten myself into. Once on the beach, the hot air. The hot towel.

My third husband.

My daughters, home before midnight and in their beds. They each come in quietly and kiss *me* goodnight. I tell them: sticks feathers string mud. They understand.

Asian American Lit. Final

Choose three and answer in short essays:

1. Disease is an important literal and figurative element in Carlos Bulosan's landmark novel, *America Is in the Heart.* Explain.

2. In Li-Young Lee's poem, "The Cleaving," the speaker refers to many male figures (Chinatown butcher, grandfather, Emerson, Jew, and so on). What kind of dynamic does he engender within that imagery? Explain.

 *

Cocksucker, motherfucker. Thief. Wetback. Colonial pig. Explain.

lover, brother, grandfather

Shulamite

 *

3. According to Said in *Orientalism,* Flaubert created a model of the Oriental Woman that went beyond the boundaries of his own literary works to influence popular notions of *the Orient* itself. Although this man was a sex tourist in the mid-1800s, some of the exotic imagery persists today. Give an example from our readings.

 *

Dear Y—how do you teach *Dictee* in your class on the long poem?—K

Dear Y—this sounds like ruthless affirmative action—and it is—but do you use your middle name when sending out poems? No one would know from your name *what* you are. It matters.—K

 *

4. Identify which literary works the following are from:
No Name Aunt
Kiyo
Jasmine

5. What is the significance of the title, *Eat a Bowl of Tea?*

12/2

In the corridor after the final: *How can that bitch expect us to remember all those names—they're weird. You know, like different. And who cares.* What would Traise say to them—

6. Why *No-No Boy?*

7. How does the Asian American body appear in Jessica Hagedorn's poem—
In Cathy Song's poem—
In Marilyn Chin's poem—
In Janice Mirikitani's poem—
In Meena Alexander's poem—
In Myung Mi Kim's poem—
            *
In Frances Chung's Chinatown—
In Fay Chiang's—
            *
In Lois Ann Yamanaka's Hawai'i—

12/2 continued

Asked an editor if they'd be interested in an anthology on Asian American women and madness—like Hisaye's characters—

In Nellie Wong's—
In Mitsuye Yamada's—

12/2 continued

Do I recycle images hoping they will endlessly ignite? Do we all recycle them? make our own clichés?

12/2 continued

S said she's not sure about high school—at the entrance test, the girls were standing on line in ethnic clots. *Where do I fit in? I don't look Asian the way they do.* Neither do I.

*

12/5

I am proposing a course on how Asian American writers react to the image of the Asian Other. Title: Sex and the "Oriental."

Notes

Must reread Shawn and Nora's books. And catch up on next generation.

Notes

Relation to the English language involves betrayal and adoration—like Latino writers except they have two (Spanish *and* Portuguese) in the mix. Asian Americans have dozens—plus dialects. Plus class and gender differences in speech.

anata
kimi

8. In 1989 Trinh suggested "a triple bind" for women of color. Is this still a valid grievance? How and how not—give examples from *Charlie Chan Is Dead.*

9. According to the Styles section, "ethnic ambiguity" is the new thing. State your own opinion.

*

In Marie Hara's—
In Mei-mei Berssenbrugge's—
In Ai's—
     *

    12/7

Probably not cool to add something on *Hahn's unbearable heart.*

    12/7 continued

intra-ethnic

    12/8

I plan on proposing a course on Asian American work inspired by/influenced by Asian literature. Title: Continental Drift.

Boerum Hill, Late Summer

(2002)

41

Back home, the weeds along the Gowanus Canal are not from a can
    marked "Meadow Flowers"—though I recognize a few stalks,
    sharp as nerves.

Shelling

I wouldn't know about cocoons, hives, egg sacs, burrows. I
wouldn't know.

TO: magma@mindset.com
This is the apartment without men. Without trousers or socks left
on the floor. Damp towels. Without electric razor. Without the miss-
ing remote. This is the apartment men visit. And every morning we
three sit at my ridiculously retro yellow kitchen table—the one girl
splitting a bagel with me, the other munching cold cereal. Opening
the paper, we read the horoscopes—Pisces, Sagittarius, Cancer—then
"Mutts" and "Get Fuzzy." In such a daze of comfort, rituals rise pun-
gent as yeasty dough. Can you tell I'm happy?
REPLY:
Hey you niche of happiness—you ought to add "Doonesbury" just
to have one without talking animals.
REPLY:
Ok ok—guess I'm pretty transparent.

I think of this summer and I think of trying to enforce curfews.
Ah, my wily little weeds! Please come home to sleep!

FM: magma@mindset.com
Or "Boondocks."

By chance, the taxi turns through Prospect Park and it is red,
this autumn, this dusk of feeling so little. Now I'm home.

Two stories below, a shopkeeper opens the superette gate and
the F rumbles passed. And where does loss reside?

      *

TO: harolds@mindset.com
Thank you for the Chinatown coffee cup—I found the package in
the cupboard this morning—as you had planned. I stood there for

a moment not sure if I had hidden a gift from the children. You are so sweet—it's such a special dark pink, and special too are those bats and the *longevity* character. Thank you thank you! Wish you were here to sip from it.
REPLY:
With you in my arms. On my lap. Missing you, honeycake.

I think of this summer and I think of our rented cottage: filled with shadows, cool as a mother's palm against a fever.

pomegranate, poppy, pod—

10.1.00

To turn off all sound by turning on the shower's noise. The comfort of scalding water. Of cleansing steam. When all else fails as home, I take a shower.

10.2.00

Spent afternoon in bed with H—reading, being read to and touching at every moment. Love to have that man here. I no longer feel like *the bottomless pit* of my ex's grievances—like *a problem*. At the same time I have a new feeling of home with my girls. Both feelings of home exquisitely grounding.

*

It's time to go home—out of the cold rain so long mistaken for a version of comfort. Was my key that lost?

As I drive past tent caterpillars along Route 80, I think of the former husband—and despise that former self for remaining so silent.

*

10.3.00

Here I can tend to strength—to be a decent mother. Although I am just now trying to write a poem about the archetypal Terrible Mother. Working title: "The Closet." Intrigued by how each mother is both the ideal and stepmother. Exhausting. H thinks it's coming along. S loves the language. One of my notes includes a paraphrase of Campbell's work on primitive mythology: "In fact her name [Mother Earth]: *Mater—materies—matrix*—means 'matter.' " I am finally full of rage at myself. Finally. It was only a year ago he threatened to take the house and the children.

     *

waquarium@mic.hawaii.edu.MLP

"Despite the protection of their borrowed shells, they are preyed upon by larger hermit crabs, box crabs, octopus, as well as wrasses and other reef fishes with jaws for crushing shelled invertebrates."

shirt, dress, coat/veil, shield—

My daughter brings a pumpkin from her father's girlfriend's moldering field and I would like to drop it from the window. See it splatter. Except it is from a child's hands.

pond, lake, spring—

TO: magma@mindset.com

When we were little, what did you think of my family—you were hardly over since we played mostly in your well-stocked attic?
REPLY:
Your house *was* strange. Both our families liked weird art so all the masks and Dürer's "Adam and Eve" (naked people!) didn't seem unusual. But it felt like there were no doors. No separate rooms.
REPLY:

I'm trying to recall which daughter asked last year if we could always live in this tiny rental because it's so comfy? It's true—it's the atmosphere. A nest in a tall tree.

"Sticks feathers string mud," I would say then kiss the child goodnight. And here I am deep in mud.

10.5.00

At a thrift shop this afternoon I found a black-lace strapless gown, floor length, perfect fit. I bought it for J & W's wedding. I'll add the Tiffany necklace H gave me for my birthday. Amazing: I feel whole in two different ways. One sexual—woman and girl. The other differently sexual—mother. Both very female and not mutually exclusive—just the emphasis different.

*

The canal remains the same green strip except for slats of ice as vague as homesick.

nest, cradle, bed, ship, wagon, coffin

*

10.5.00 continued

I remember a poetry reading out-of-town and seeing a former lover. When he left my hotel room, I felt so homesick. Sick to my stomach. I wish I could recall what I did to overcome it.

The canal remains the same except for the accidental lilacs. But that was spring. Now who will know their scent?

*

10.5.00

Where is my art in all this? If only I could sit for a moment and

take a breath. Catch my breath. My poems are one-line long, after
Hiro's translations of Shikishi.

   *

Journal entry from 3.10.99

This afternoon H heard something in my voice and asked me,
What's wrong? Anything wrong? And I said, *I miss my mother. But I think
I've always missed my mother.* Sometimes I just lie down on the floor
and cry, *Mommy Mommy.*

Journal entry from 6.23.91

He asks *not* to be touched.

   *

barrel, box, basket, chest, trough, sack

cave, temple, hut, house, lattice, fence, wall, gate and door

10.7.00

She is weeping with her face in her pillow. I tell her boys turn atten-
tion to boys and work/sports; girls turn to the "phone," that is, to
waiting. If maturing is, in part, about subversion and identity—then
is it also about learning not to wait for men? (Although I have to
admit I still talk with M about waiting.) On another note, I'm look-
ing for a science journal article on extremophiles. Also the name of
that bird that lays eggs in other nests. Well—this is not about waiting.

pig, shellfish, squid, owl

   *

I feel luscious to his lips, even—or especially in this bitter light
  in his office on the industrial carpet.

*

10.7.00 continued

They begin as my own bleeding wanes. And yet I feel more fertile—
not to bear children, but to create powerfully. On the other hand—J
and her partner brought their baby girl over yesterday and the two
women lavished such warmth that I wished I were their daughter.

waquarium@mic.hawaii.edu.MLP
"The larvae feed and grow as they drift in ocean currents. When
they have reached the right stage of development, they drop to the
seafloor and metamorphose into their bottom-dwelling form and
must immediately find a small snail shell for protection."

Postcard from Summer [unsent]

Dear S—working on the piece for your book in our little rented cot-
tage. A funny incident in the bay: one hermit crab wanted a bigger
shell (of course), even if just slightly roomier. He dragged a shell
away from the other smaller ones and began to tug out the dead
remains. Tough work. Soon there was an audience—after all, there's
little else to do and what if this one didn't fit? so much the better to
be next in line! Let the big guy do the work. It was hysterically
funny and I spent about twenty minutes watching until H pulled
me away to go home for lunch. More later—K

    *

Outside the train window every thing is brown—but all differ-
    ent browns. I imagine growing very old with him and
    knock my head, "knocking wood."

Outside this train window is a salt marsh and I think of the
    day Mother died and I think of the man the train is

speeding towards. And the marsh is both sorrow and relief, at once.

     *

10.8.00 phone message

Sweetie—the land hermit crab you bought me rearranged all his "furniture" over night! Guess the extra shell and cactus log were in the wrong corners! Call me—I need to hear your voice.

     *

FM: magma@mindset.com

Home is so moveable for you. Probably more about identity than a location.

REPLY:

Another friend asked me what will happen to my sense of home when I have a man back in these rooms. I wonder.

Conspiring with Shikishi

tanka inspired by Shikishi and her predecessors
—with grateful acknowledgment to the translator, Hiroaki Sato—

i.

Looking at the moon, I feel sad in a thousand ways, though the
  autumn isn't mine alone —Oe no Chisato

Evening mist forming in the depths of my heart, the autumn as it
  wanes is mine alone —Shikishi

The evening mist dampens his heart, I know. He will not see his
  way through *this missed.*

The evening mists and my face is wet—ah, to be both mother and
  daughter, bereft.

The evening mist forming in my heart: the one daughter runs off
  into that dark. The other watches.

ii.

Loneliness is the habit of this house: I gaze at the leaves with frost
  spread over them —Shikishi

Loneliness is the habit of this apartment—this bowl of flowers that,
  outside, would still root in the frost.

Spring is the habit of this apartment: each morning I rub the mist
  off the bathroom mirror so I can see us both brushing and
  gargling.

iii.

The reality of the dark, of leopard-flower seeds, wasn't at all better
than reliable dreams! —Anonymous from Kokinshū
Not even knowing the reality of the fleeting dark, I wander along
from dream to dream —Shikishi

The reality of day lilies twisting into brown froth—I can cry for my
mother in any season.

The seeds of those leopard flowers I do not know—nor what takes
root in your breast that you pluck out—in order to live with
me, my daughter.

iv.

Painful to think of her without her knowing it: I wish it would
show in color like the safflower!
—Anonymous from Kokinshū

My sleeves are wet and I keep this secret, yet how would I deal with
the safflower? —Shikishi

Painful to think the safflower already knows: soon I will leave one
man for the other.

v.

You must have seen the high plum branches of my house; so unex-
pected has been your visit   '—Taira no Kanemori

At my house, since high plum branches flowered I've been waiting,
though for whom I can't say   —Shikishi

The blossoms on the highest plum branch cannot be seen from
here—but the daughter who looks back may recall them in
years to come.

The blossoms on the highest plum branch—I can just see them. I
can worry about her distance.

The uppermost plum blossoms cannot be clipped—except by the
downpour forecast and arriving. I wish she were home.

She writes of the highest branch—but what are they—those
blossoms?

vii.

I'm waiting, I tell others, for the moon to rise above the foot-
wearying mountain, but it's for you I wait
                              —Anonymous from Manyōshū

Waiting for you I do not go into my bedroom. Do not shine on its
cypress door long, moon near the hills   —Shikishi

Who cares about the moon after all—the street lamp over the
corner pay phone is bright till dawn.

Who cares about the moon over the skyline—who cares about
him—and who cares about what I thought was my heart—

Notes

"Compass" was gleaned from a talk I gave: "Disorder as Order." Although I had read and reread the zuihitsu of Sei Shōnagon (and Kenkō) for many years, I am in debt to Ed Friedman for inviting me to actually try my hand at writing one—maybe two decades ago—for a celebration of her work at The Poetry Project at St. Mark's Church. Also to Margaret Holly for turning my attention to *Formless in Form: Kenkō, "Tsurezuregusa," and the Rhetoric of Japanese Fragmentary Prose* by Linda H. Chance, Stanford: Stanford University Press, 1997.

"Opening Her Text"

The Tale of Genji, Genjimonogatari, by Murasaki Shikibu.

Tanka

All the tanka are very loosely based on the form, which in Japanese is thirty-one syllables. Although I have not maintained the count, I have attempted brevity, the original convention of rendering each as a single line, and the use of seasonal/nature references.

"Radio and Mirror"

This is a completely subjective response to Abe Kobo's *The Woman in the Dunes, Suna no onna* which was translated by E. Dale Saunders.

"Sparrow"

The Narrow Road to the North, Oku no hosomichi, by Bashō Matsuo.
This zuihitsu was originally published by *XCP* with a different series of poems based on bridge crossings. They finally felt too literal and so I substituted a series that used quotes by Charles Wright as triggering lines; the lines themselves have fallen by the wayside.

"The Tunnel"

This is a completely subjective response to *Snow Country, Yukiguni,* by Kawabata Yasunari, which was exquisitely translated by Edward G. Seidensticker. The bold and italicized words and lines are from his translation.

"Pulse and Impulse"

This is a revised version of a piece originally written for a collection on motherhood and poetics.

"Blunt Instrument"

This is a revised version of a piece originally written for the collection *After Confession*.

"Trading Words"

The bold and italicized words and lines are from W. H. Auden's "September 1, 1939."

"Firsts in No Particular Order"

Many thanks to Laure-Anne Bosselaar and Kurt Brown for this "assignment"!

"Shelling"

Written in response to Suzanne Fiol's portrait of my two daughters and me.

"Conspiring with Shikishi"

I am responding to the Japanese tradition of literary allusion. The italicized tanka in each section are from *String of Beads: Complete Poems of Princess Shikishi*, translated by Hiroaki Sato, Honolulu: University of Hawaii Press, 1993. This has been an immensely crucial text for me and I hope that Hiro's ears have been buzzing wildly!

Acknowledgments

I am grateful to those writers who have encouraged me to pursue these forms and themes—including Mark Nowak, Laure-Anne Bosselaar, John Weir, Harold Schechter—and especially Jill Bialosky.

(And Rei—the next book is for you!)

A summer grant from my union, PSC-CUNY, assisted at a crucial time.

Also thanks to the editors of the following books and journals for taking a chance with these trials of form:

After Confession, David Graham and Kate Sontag, eds. (Graywolf Press, 2002): "Blunt Instrument"

BOMB: "Opening Her Text" and several tanka

Columbia: "Cuts from the Zuihitsu on My Daughter" and several tanka

Indiana Review: "Conspiring with Shikishi"

Monolid: "Things that Make Me Cry Instantly"

New Writings on Motherhood and Poetics, Brenda Hillman and Patricia Dienstfrey, eds. (University of California Press, 2002): "Pulse and Impulse: the Zuihitsu"

Never Before: poems on first experiences, Laure-Anne Bosselaar and Kurt Brown, eds. (Four Way Books, 2005): "First in No Particular Order"

Xcp [cross cultural poetics]: "The Orient," "Utica Station, Dep 10:07 a.m. to N.Y. Penn Station," "Sparrow"

Washington Square: "Radio and Mirror"

A number of the tanka have also appeared in the following journals: *Audrey, The Clarion, Hanging Loose, rattapallax*; and in the following anthologies: Ulrich Baer, ed. *110 Stories: New York Writes after September 11* (New York University Press); William Heyen, ed. *September 11, 2001: American writers respond* (Etruscan Press); Dennis Joy Johnson and Valerie Merians, eds. *Poetry after 9/11: an anthology of New York poets* (Melville House)